Table Of Contents

Introduction

The Gay Travel Guide For Tops And Bottoms – USA Edition was one of the more controversial and harder projects that my one best top friend and my one best bottom friend encountered—so much so that we had to add a "swing" vote and consult local drag queens to get their opinions. This is because we would say the USA as a whole would probably skew very versatilely (is that a word?).

Since I was assigned to interviewing each city's local drag talent, I can say it was "no picnic"—those bitches don't give anything away for free. I feel I need to write a book, "Cities With The Bitchiest Drag Queens" (Seattle would win), but I'd rather honor those drag queens who were very professional, helpful, and nice. So, here's a shout out to Detox Icunt of West Hollywood, California and Miss Victoria Secret (Vickki West) of San Francisco, California. They went above the call of duty and were really helpful in our research.

The United States as a whole is really beginning (albeit slowly) to recognize the importance of gay rights. We have seen the removal of Don't Ask Don't Tell (DADT), which prohibited gays from serving honorably in the US Military. We have also seen the beginnings of the repeal of the Defense of Marriage Act (DOMA), which will probably be removed within the next couple of years, allowing for gays who are married to freely move within the USA without restrictions.

That having been said, there are places in the USA that are friendly towards the LGBT Community and there are places that are not.

On a down note, the US economy is in dire straits (pardon the pun), so this is our effort to help bring travel to the most optimal destinations. We do give preference to "gay owned" establishments, so if we missed one please let us know. Our most favorite "gay owned" restaurant is Orphan Andy's in San Francisco. I went to university in San Francisco (long ago when

Jesus had only three apostles) and have many fond memories of eating there.

Do keep in mind that it is common policy at bars and nightclubs in the USA to check for identification. So please make sure you take your passport or driver's license when you go out.

Enjoy!
Drew Blancs

2. CALIFORNIA

California is rich in gay US history. From the first meeting of the Mattachine Society in Los Angeles in 1950, to West Hollywood being the first gay incorporated city, California is the birthplace of the gay rights movement. Until recently, the state had been one of the most progressive in advocating for gay rights. California is considered generally liberal in its policies regarding the LGBT community. The legal rights of lesbian, gay, bisexual and transgender people have dramatically improved since 1960 at both the state and municipal level. The state grants extensive recognition to same-sex couples, one of the first states to have done so. California briefly legalized gay marriage at one point, but a referendum (Proposition 8) stopped any new marriages from occurring. The issue is now in US Federal Courts and at this time, a conclusive decision has not been made.

With its movie industry, temperate weather, and many tourist sites, California is a favorite for gay tourists worldwide. Our two travelers have voted California to be the state with the fittest men and the most fun. West Hollywood bars on any given afternoon have patios which become lively. In general, the fun starts at 1pm and lasts until the wee hours of the morning.

Our Bottom Traveler – (rating 3 out of 5) Tops are VERY rare in West Hollywood, but I persisted and I was able to find one. Notice I said *find* one; not *enjoy* one.
Our Top Traveler – (rating 5 out of 5) This guy wanted me to guarantee that I was bigger than 8 inches. So, on a cocktail napkin, I drew two circles (one small and one big). I pointed to the smaller one and said this is your asshole BEFORE having sex with me. Let's just say he picked up my bar tab and we were back in my hotel room in under 5 minutes.

ACCOMMODATIONS

Ramada Plaza Hotel Suites West Hollywood/Beverly Hills
8585 Santa Monica Blvd.
West Hollywood, CA 90069 US
Phone: (310) 652-6400
Reservation: 1-800-845-8585

http://www.ramadaweho.com/

As so attractively put on their website, the Ramada invites you to:
"Sit back, relax and enjoy your stay at our Ramada Plaza Hotel
Suites West Hollywood/Beverly Hills. Located off Route 101 on
the outskirts of the Hollywood Hills, our West Hollywood hotel
provides a comforting break after a day of big-city excitement.
Kick your shoes off and watch your flat-screen TV or surf the
web using free Wi-Fi Internet access. Take a dip in our outdoor
pool or lounge on our sundeck. Get a workout in our fitness
center, and then rejuvenate with products available at Body
Factory."

Andaz West Hollywood
8401 Sunset Boulevard
West Hollywood, California
90069
USA
Tel: (323) 656-1234
Fax: (323) 650-7024
http://www.westhollywood.andaz.hyatt.com/hyatt/hotels/index.js
p?offerId=24

The Andaz West Hollywood offers the following description of
their services on their website: "When you stay with us, realize
that you're finding more than just a place to lay your head.
You've found a home on the road – a familiar friend whose
mantra is 'my home is yours.' From the moment you walk into
Andaz West Hollywood, you'll notice the difference – a refined

7

and relaxed check in process that is located in a space that feels more like a living room than a hotel lobby. Walk through the doors of the hotel, located on the chic Sunset Boulevard, and you'll be immediately greeted by one of our Andaz Hosts."

The Parker Guest House
520 Church Street
San Francisco, California 94114
TOLL FREE: 1-888-520-7275
info@parkerguesthouse.com
http://www.parkerguesthouse.com/

As written on their website: "The Parker Guest House, a San Francisco gay 21 room Hotel/Bed and Breakfast, hosts both gay and straight guests and is the most highly rated gay hotel and gay bed and breakfast in San Francisco's vibrant Castro District. This Castro inn and Mission District hotel is the top ranked San Francisco gay resort according to Damron, GayCities.com and Sparticus travel guides, as well as many others."

RESTAURANTS

Bossa Nova
685 N. Robertson Blvd.
West Hollywood, California 90069
Tel: (310) 657-5070
Fax: (310) 657-0358
http://www.bossanovafood.com/site/index.cfm

Sunday thru Thursday from 11:00am to 12:00am
Friday and Saturday from 11:00am to 4:00am
Parking: Public parking available next South door at all times of
operation.

Popular amongst natives and tourists alike, this bistro offers a
diverse menu to fit any food-lover's palate. Its convenient
location makes it perfect for a pre-bar meal or even a post-bar
snack.

Hamburger Mary's
8288 Santa Monica Blvd.
West Hollywood, CA 90046
Tel: (323) 654-3800
Fax: (323) 654-3808
http://hamburgermarys.com/weho/

Hamburger Mary's is open
11:00am to 1:00am
Sunday through Thursday.
Open until 2:00am
Friday and Saturday.

"Eat drink and be. . .MARY!" boasts this campy burger chain.
Known for more than just its burgers, patrons will delight at its
frequent drink specials, Taco Tuesdays, and Bingo Wednesdays.
Hamburger Mary's is a must-visit for anyone in staying the
WeHo area.

Orphan Andy's
3991 17th Street (Castro Street)
San Francisco, CA 94114
Tel: (415) 864-9795

Check out what Orphan Andy's has to say on its website: "Sober up or kill a hangover at this greasy spoon. A Castro institution, Andy's fills up when the bars close and can provide some classic people watching. Standard diner fare round-the-clock keeps the mo's coming back."

NIGHTLIFE

Micky's
8857 Santa Monica Blvd.
West Hollywood, CA 90069
(310) 657-1176
http://www.mickys.com

Happy Hour 4-9 p.m.

Not cooling off even after its building fire, this hot WeHo club is
the place to be on any given weekend. With a fully stacked bar,
attractive clientele of both sexes, and now a menu full of
delicious eats, Micky's is a vibrant destination for any traveler.

SF Badlands
4121 18th St. (Castro)
San Francisco, CA 94114
Tel: (415) 626-9320
http://www.badlands-sf.com/

Happy Hour (cocktails 2 for 1) Monday - Saturday 3-8 pm and
our popular Beer Busts every Sunday 2-8 pm.

In their own words, "SF Badlands is the Castro's most popular
location for video/music entertainment and dancing. Our dance
floor features a state-of-the-art EAW-powered sound system, and
colorful dance floor lighting with a traditional rotating mirror
ball. Our front room lounge area is a great place to meet people or
hang out with your friends and enjoy the music videos."

The Café
(NOTE: It's next to the Chevron Gas Station)
2367 Market St. (Castro & 17th)
San Francisco, CA 94114
Tel: (415) 861-3846
http://www.cafésf.com

Open nightly till 2am

Once the only place to dance in the Castro, this club maintains its prime reputation to this day. Its huge, renovated dance floor is constantly packed with both boys and girls, and its mid-bar courtyard makes it one of the Castro's most lively locations. Weekend clubbers will often find a line to get in thanks to fabulous promotion nights like Boy Bar Fridays. This makes The Café one of the hottest spots to hit in the area.

3. FLORIDA

Florida has been slow in granting rights to same sex couples, and it was only until recently that the 33 year old ban on gay adoptions was lifted by the state courts. Florida became famous in the 1970s, as Anita Bryant, a Florida orange juice spokesperson, spearheaded campaigns against gay rights. Her outspoken public views caused the Florida Citrus Commission to allow her contract to lapse. This was due, in part, to a gay-led drive to boycott Florida orange juice. Since 2008, Florida has enacted a law which bans the recognition of same-sex marriages in the state.

However, Florida's warm climate, sunny beaches, and gay hot spots like Miami Beach, Orlando, and Ft. Lauderdale make it a gay travel mecca. The traveling duo went to Orlando and stayed at a "resort" called the Parliament House. If you're in town for unique sex, the Parliament House is a "must see" on any gay Florida trip.

Our Bottom Traveler – (rating 4 out of 5) After a few drinks, this guy said, "I'm gonna rape your ass." Of course, I replied, "You can't rape the willing, but you can try anyway."

Our Top Traveler – (rating 4 out of 5) I had a lot of choices in every city we went to in Florida. I'm not gonna say these guys had loose assholes, but when I went to rim one, I swear I heard an echo down there.

FLORIDA

ACCOMMODATIONS

Ed Lugo Resort
2404 NE 8 Ave (Wilton Drive and NE 8 Ave)
Fort Lauderdale, Fl 33305
Wilton Manors
Tel: (954) 275-8299
http://www.edlugoresort.com/

Check out what the Ed Lugo Resort has to say about its cozy establishment: "Conveniently located in Fort Lauderdale, Ed Lugo Resort offers easy access to South Beach, Port Everglades, Miami and all the excitement South Florida offers. A short 10 minute drive to the Fort Lauderdale airport or to your Fort Lauderdale cruise ship port. Luxury features like always-heated pool, waterfalls, beautiful landscaping and 500 count luxury sheets make Ed Lugo Resort the place to relax."

The Grand Resort and Spa
539 North Birch Road
Ft. Lauderdale, FL 33304
Toll-free: 1-800-818-1211
Tel: (954) 630-3000
Fax: (954) 630-3003
E-mail: info@grandresort.net
http://grandresort.net/

Here's a little bit about The Grand Resort and Spa courtesy of their website: "The Grand Resort and Spa is Fort Lauderdale Beach's largest and finest gay owned and operated men's resort hotel, located just steps from the beach and convenient to all the attractions and nightlife for which Ft. Lauderdale is now world renowned."

Lords South Beach at Nash
1120 Collins Avenue
Miami Beach, FL 33139
Tel: (877) 448-4754|(305) 674-7800

reservations@lordssouthbeach.com
http://www.lordssouthbeach.com/

Located just minutes from the most popular beach spot in all of South Beach, the Lords South Beach Hotel is a paragon destination for gay travelers. Visitors will fall in love with its bohemian style interior, friendly staff, and exciting attractions—posh dining, a sexy night life, and so much more. Lords South Beach Hotel is a definite must for lovers of the good life.

RESTAURANTS

Rosie's Bar & Grill
2449 Wilton Drive
Wilton Manor, FL 33305
Tel: (954) 563-0123
http://www.rosiesbarandgrill.com/

A nucleus at the center of the Wilton Manors community, Rosie's proves itself as much more than your average burger joint. Diners will surely enjoy the effervescent multi-colored lights on the patio during this restaurant's gay-scene power lunches, and will love looking their best at Sunday Brunch! A delicious menu filled with burgers, steaks, and salads makes Rosie's a great stop anytime.

Humpy's
2244 Wilton Drive
Wilton Manors, FL 33305
Tel: (954) 566-2722
http://www.humpyspizza.com/

Sun-Wed 11am-10pm
Thurs-Sat 11am-2am

Ever stay out late and just can't shake that craving for pizza? Humpy's has got you covered, conveniently located in the same shopping plaza as Georgie's Alibi and Atomic Boom. And if you happen to love the sweeter side of things, one look at their cupcake cooler will be enough to make you go wild!

Balan's
1022 Lincoln Rd. (Lenox)
Miami Beach, FL 33139
Upper Eastside
Tel: (305) 534-9191
http://www.balans.co.uk/Whats_new_Miami.php
Sun-Thu 8am-12am, Fri/Sat 8am-1am

With patio seating, good prices, and better cocktails, this gay-friendly location will make your eyes widen. Stop by for breakfast so you can catch an eyeful when the men of South Beach show up with their best fresh look.

NIGHTLIFE

Georgie's Alibi
2266 Wilton Dr. (NE 6th Ave.)
Fort Lauderdale, FL 33305
Wilton Manors
Tel : (954) 565-2526
http://www.georgiesalibi.com/

Open Daily till 2am
3am Fridays and Saturdays

Renowned bar Georgie's Alibi is something for everyone. A video bar, restaurant/café, and sports bar all wrapped up in one, it has become known as the unofficial heart of Wilton Manors. Stop by on the weekend or even on a Thursday, when their $3 Long Island Ice Teas will make you feel nice and loose in good company.

The Manor
2345 Wilton Dr.
Fort Lauderdale, FL 33305
Wilton Manors
(954) 626-0082
info@themanorcomplex.com
http://www.themanorcomplex.com

The spitting image of "The Abbey" in West Hollywood, The
Manor's spacious interior serves as a great hangout for friends.
Also a venue for comedy shows and well-known singers, their
notoriously sweaty dance floor will leave you hot and satisfied.
Perfect for younger crowds, The Manor is a great spot to check
out in Wilton Manors.

Twist
1057 Washington Ave.
Miami Beach, FL 33139
South Beach
(305) 53T-WIST
http://www.twistsobe.com/

Open until late weekends

Here's Twist according to Twist: "TWIST is the infamous South
Beach gay club, known throughout the world for its great music,
friendly staff, and always being packed with hot tourists and
locals alike. TWIST is actually seven bars in one with each bar
having its own unique atmosphere and décor. You can literally
"bar hop" without ever leaving this two story club. TWIST is
open seven days a week from 1pm to 5am. Its motto is its mantra
- Never a Cover - Always a Groove. Its reputation as a "must do"
when in Miami is well deserved."

4. GEORGIA

Georgia has very few LGBT rights compared to other more progressive states in the country. In fact, it has only been since 1998 that their sodomy laws were removed by court order. Since 2004, there has been an amendment prohibiting recognition of same-sex marriages at the state level.

However, Atlanta has a thriving gay population and is known for its fantastic night life, restaurants and hotels.

Georgia is a very scenic state and rich in US history, especially when it comes to the US Civil War Era. It is known as the "Peach State" for its vibrant peach and fruit industry.

Our Bottom Traveler – (rating 4 out of 5) After sex, this guy said I reminded him of his brother. This made the moment VERY AWKWARD.

Our Top Traveler – (rating 4 out of 5) I had a lot of fun in Atlanta. I brought home two guys who were friends and both bottoms. A good time was had by all.

GEORGIA

ACCOMMODATIONS

W Atlanta Midtown
188 14th St. NE (Juniper St. NE)
Atlanta, GA 30361
Midtown
Tel: (404) 892-6000
http://www.starwoodhotels.com/whotels/property/overview/index
.html?propertyID=3131

The W Atlanta Midtown can be found between Piedmont Park
and Midtown Mile. Its attractive location in the middle of the
"Hotlanta" zone makes it a good choice for creatures of the night
and lovers of culture!

Hotel Indigo
683 Peachtree St. NE
Atlanta, GA 30308
Toll Free: 1-866-2INDIGO
Tel: (404) 874-9200
Fax: (404) 874-4245

Check-In: 3:00 p.m.
Check-Out: 12:00 p.m.

The Hotel Indigo boats a radiantly designed interior which gives
off an aura of dazzling brightness and space. Classy travelers will
love its proximity to the arts district and the famous Fox Theatre,
and dog owners will delight at their daily Canine Cocktail Hour!

Park Avenue Manor
107-109 West Park Avenue, Savannah, GA
Tel: (912) 233-0352
Email: info(@)parkavenuemanor.com
http://www.parkavenuemanor.com/

For travelers seeking that hospitable, southern touch, the cozy Park Avenue Manor is definitely their cup of tea. Ranging from free Wi-Fi to complementary brownies and sherry, the endless amenities at the Park Avenue Manor will leave you happily contented. Take note of the pink and purple décor at the entrance: it shows that this hotel is definitely gay friendly!

RESTAURANTS

Cowtippers Steaks & Spirits
1600 Piedmont Ave
Atlanta GA 30324
Tel: (404) 874-3751
Fax: (404) 875-1666
cowtippers@metrocafés.com e-mail
http://metrocafés.com/Cowtippers/Home.aspx

The laid back, casual atmosphere of this steakhouse is surpassed only by its delicious food_burgers, fries, salads, and amazingly huge Texas Margaritas! Check it out for lunch or dinner.

Joe's on Juniper
1049 Juniper Street
Atlanta, GA 30309
Tel: (404) 875-6634
Fax: (404) 892-1568
joesonjuniper@metrocafés.com
http://metrocafés.com/joes-juniper/Home.aspx

Go to Joe's for the hot wings, calamari, and martinis_you won't be disappointed. This extremely popular joint has a strong midtown following and an even stronger, livelier atmosphere!

Papillote
218 West Broughton Street
Savannah, GA 31401
Tel : (912) 232-1881
Fax : (912) 238-1883
info@papillote-savannah.com
http://papillote-savannah.com/

Hours of Operation:
Tuesday: 10:30 AM to 4:00 PM
Wednesday – Saturday: 10:30 AM to 7:00 PM
Sunday: 12:00 PM to 5:00 PM

Monday: closed

This French bistro, conceived by an innovative and entrepreneurial couple, brings passion and charm to the fine dining experience. Its varied menu and beautiful décor will satisfy even the most stringent of critics!

NIGHTLIFE

Swinging Richards
1400 Northside Dr. NW (Reservoir Dr. NW)
Atlanta, GA 30318
Midtown
Tel: (404) 352-0532
http://www.swingingrichards.com/

Tues-Sat, 6:30 p.m. - 3 a.m.
Sun–Mon, Closed

There's a reason the U.S.'s largest male dancer bar is called "Swinging Richards". This Atlanta hotspot features fully nude exotic dancers on several stages and even VIP rooms for private shows. Sailors and Soldiers delight: this club offers free admission with a Military ID!

Blake's on the Park
227 10th Street NE
Atlanta, GA 30309
Tel: (404) 892-5786

Monday - Friday: 11:00am - 3:00am
Saturday: 2:00pm - 3:00am
Sunday: 2:00pm - 12:00am

This local joint is a fantastic place to find a boy before a night clubbing on the town. There may be no dance floor, but the weeknight drag shows definitely draw many from the twenty-thirty something crowd!

Club One
1 Jefferson Street
Savannah, GA 31401
Tel: (912) 232-0200
http://www.clubone-online.com

Perhaps the biggest and most well known gay club in Savannah, Club One is host to the monthly Lady Chablis drag show. With features such as a spacious dance floor, a basement video bar, and drag shows, this club is a must visit for every party-lover.

5. ILLINOIS

Illinois is surprisingly progressive on the issues of LGBT rights. They have a statewide domestic partner program, hate crime laws, and anti-discrimination laws that include the LGBT Community.

However, Illinois still has a statute that prohibits the recognition of same-sex marriages. Recent polls show that Illinois is evenly split on granting same sex partners the right to marry.

Of course, in Illinois is the city of Chicago, which is unanimously (amongst our author and two gay travelers) a "MUST SEE" city for gay US travels.

Our Bottom Traveler – (rating 5 out of 5) I would say that the sex saunas are the nicest and cleanest in the USA. I know most bottoms want to find the city with the most tops but I have to say the BEST SEX I have ever had was in Chicago.

Our Top Traveler – (rating 5 out of 5) I have to say that Chicago is my most favorite city in terms of fun, friendliness, and overall travel. I actually considered abandoning our USA tour because I fell for a guy in this city. So, Chicago has my heart.

ILLINOIS

ACCOMMODATIONS

Villa Toscana
3447 N. Halsted Street (Roscoe St.)
Chicago, IL 60657
(Boystown)
Tel 1: (773) 404-2643
Tel 2: (800) 404-2643
http://www.thevillatoscana.com/

If you're looking for varied, antique charm, Villa Toscana is definitely the place for you. Their numerous suites (such as the Neo-Classic, Venetian, and Moroccan) have something for every visitor. Its central, convenient location makes it a good choice for city explorers!

Best Western Hawthorne Terrace
3434 North Broadway
Chicago, IL 60657
Boystown
Tel 1: (773) 244-3434
Tel 2: (888) 860-3400
http://www.hawthorneterrace.com

With its familiar reliable name, this Best Western certainly doesn't disappoint. Located at the heart of Boystown, this cozy chain is surely a great choice.

Allegro Chicago
171 West Randolph Street
Chicago, IL 60601
North Loop
Reservations: 1-800-643-1500
Tel: (312) 236-0123
Fax: (312) 236-0917
http://www.allegrochicago.com

For those adventurers who want to get out and experience the city, the Allegro is situated at the center of a large variety of theatres and shopping complexes. Featuring beautiful Art Deco rooms, amenities such as a full service spa, a 24-hour fitness center, yoga classes, and pet-friendly packages, this hotel proves to be an excellent spot for those who love to relax and self-pamper.

RESTAURANTS

Halsted's Bar and Grill
3441 N Halsted St.
Chicago, IL 60657
Boystown
Tel: (773) 348-9696
http://www.halstedschicago.com/

Daily till 12am (Fri and Sat till 1am)

Halsted's is a great place in the wintertime thanks to its tasty burgers, sizeable salads, and large wine selection. However, what really makes it shine is its tempting outdoor beer garden, which fills up with great clients in the summer.

Firefly
3335 N Halsted St.
Chicago, IL 60657
Boystown
Tel: (773) 525-2505
http://fireflyonhalsted.com/

Daily till 130am (Midnight on Sunday)

Chicago travelers looking for a French Bistro twist will be delighted by this modern American variant. Located right in the middle of lively Boystown, patrons are advised to try their mussels, their martinis, and to enjoy the great crowd.

Yoshi's Café
3257 N. Halsted
Chicago, IL 60657
Boystown
Tel: (773) 248-6160
yoshi@yoshiscafé.com

http://www.yoshiscafé.com/yoshiscafé/

Daily till 10:30pm. Closed Mondays.

As evidenced by their name, Yoshi's Café serves a wonderful combination of dishes from the Asian and French cuisines. A popular spot for vegetarians and meat-lovers alike, Yoshi's is a great spot (and well known for it) for a romantic outing.

Sidetrack
3349 N. Halsted St. (Between Roscoe and Buckingham)
Chicago, IL 60657
Boystown
Tel: (773) 477-9189
http://www.sidetrackchicago.com/

While you're staying in Boystown, this poppy dance joint is a definite must see. Featuring attractions such as video-lined walls, a rooftop beer garden in warmer months, and an awesome balcony, it makes sense that it's one of the biggest, most popular dance bars in the city.

Roscoe's
3356 N. Halsted St. (Roscoe)
Chicago, IL 60657
Boystown
Tel: (773) 281-3355
http://www.roscoes.com/

Daily till 2am (till 3am Sat)

Roscoe's is the perfect choice for the younger party-loving crowd. Hungrier clients will enjoy the attached café next door, and outdoorsy types will love the patio during the summer. Be sure to stop by for the Wet Underwear contest hosted by Friday Lay on the last Thursday of each month!

Club Traz
213 East Main Street
Carbondale, Il 62901
Tel: (618) 547-4270
http://clubtraz.com/

Informally known as the quintessential gay club in Carbondale, Club Traz is the place to be if you want to take in the gay scene.

Drag-heavy Sundays, Karaoke Wednesdays, Salsa Thursdays, and 80's Saturdays will keep you coming back every night of the week.

6. IOWA

Iowa was the first state in the Midwest to allow gay marriage. Iowa is not as conservative as most states in the Midwest, but there are a few key areas in the state that are more gay-friendly than others.

Those four main areas are: Des Moines, Cedar Rapids, Iowa City, or the Quad Cities. The Quad Cities is a group of five cities straddling the Mississippi River on the Iowa–Illinois boundary. These cities are Davenport and Bettendorf, with Davenport being more diversified and gay friendly.

Our Bottom Traveler - (rating 2 out of 5) Yes, I asked what's the kinkiest thing you did. His reply: farm animals. After hearing that I made him wear two condoms.

Our Top Traveler - (rating 2 out of 5) So, Bottomer told me he asked his hook up what's the kinkiest thing he ever did; so I thought I should ask my guy too. No joke: same response.

(NOTE: We left Iowa early the next morning, and didn't visit a damn thing—ESPECIALLY not a farm)

IOWA

ACCOMMODATIONS

Renaissance Des Moines Savery Hotel
401 Locust Street
Des Moines, IA 50309
Tel: (515) 244-2151
E-mail: reservations@marriott.com

Cheerfully decorated, my first thought was that if I hit this lobby with a hangover, it's all over for me. I found them to be a tad bit over-priced but it was unto Marriott standards in service and decor. I picked it because it wasn't that far from the Blazing Saddle Bar.

Brown Street Inn
430 Brown Street
Iowa City, IA 52245-5805
Tel: (319) 338-0435
E-mail: info@brownstreetinn.com

We woke up to fresh baked cookies to greet us each afternoon. Examples of Bob and Mark's art collection lined the staircase to the second floor with a common theme: MEN! I like this place. They have a reading library which was fun; I hadn't touched a book since I got my new iPad. However, I did not see a copy of the Gay Travel Guide For Tops and Bottoms there. I will make sure to leave this recommendation on their comment card.

Holiday Inn Express - Collins Road
1230 Collins Road
Cedar Rapids, IA 52402
Tel: (319) 294-9407
E-mail: none

I'll admit: I picked this place because it was close to Club Basix. It's a nice Holiday Inn Express. We must admit they had cute male staff there and we both tried and failed to get a "staff member" (if you know what I mean).

Scotts Restaurant (Open 24 Hours)
1906 Blairs Ferry Rd NE
Cedar Rapids, IA 52402
Tel: (319) 550-4517
E-mail/Facebook:
http://www.facebook.com/Scottsfamilyrestaurant

It's your typical diner with typical diner food. I guess we HAD to eat somewhere.

Happy Joe's Pizza and Ice Cream
2430 Spruce Hills Drive
Bettendorf, IA 52722
Tel: (563) 359-5457
E-mail/Facebook: info@happyjoes.com

This is mid western hospitality at it's best. We had a hangover and they had scheduled three kids birthday parties in unison. We immediately took our meals to go but it was a nice place.

Splash Seafood Bar & Grill
303 Locust
Des Moines, IA, 50309
Tel: (515)244-5686
E-mail/Facebook/website: www.splash-seafood.com

According to their website, "Splash Seafood Bar & Grill is Des Moines' premier seafood restaurant. This 5 star establishment—and recipient of The DiRoNA Award—has also received The Wine Spectator Award of Excellence. Splash serves fresh seafood imported daily from Hawaii and other coastal ports. Quality service, attention to detail, extraordinary art, atmosphere, Reggae music and 9 huge salt water aquariums make this restaurant a favorite."

NIGHTLIFE

The Blazing Saddle
416 East 5th Street
Des Moines, IA 50309
Tel: (515) 246--1299
E-mail/Facebook/website: www.theblazingsaddle.com

They claim to be Des Moines, Iowa's favorite gay bar. Drag
queens, leather; you'll never know for sure what you're going to
see. Primary clientele is gay males. I saw more drag queens than
cowboys.

Club Basix
3916 1st Ave NE
Cedar Rapids, IA 52402
Contact
Tel: (319) 363-3194
E-mail/Facebook/website: http://www.facebook.com/pages/Club-
Basix/

This is your "only gay nightclub in the city" sorta place but
everyone was so friendly to us. It was obvious we were tourists.
Someone asked us if we came here to get married—we both
laughed. We really liked the clientele at Club Basix. We did have
the pick of the lot since fresh meat doesn't come here too often.

Studio 13
3 South Linn Street
Iowa City, IA 52240
Tel: (319) 338-7145
E-mail/Facebook/website: *www.*sthirteen.com/

Again, this is your "only gay nightclub in the city" sorta place but
this was where my famous "kinky sex with animal" story came
from. It's a fun young crowd of mainly university students and
some locals. It was a nice mix of gays and lesbians. My new pick
up line would be "Have you ever slept with a farm animal? No?
…Let's dance".

7. LOUISIANA

Louisiana is a mixed bag when it comes to LGBT rights. On the one hand, there *are* hate crime laws in the state statutes, as well as discrimination protections that apply to the LGBT community. However, the state does not recognize gay partnerships in any form. Louisiana also refuses to amend birth records of children born into same-sex households.

New Orleans has long been a hot spot for gay travelers. It's funny to note that the now removed anti-sodomy statutes used to have a clause excluding the "mardi gras" holidays.

Our Bottom Traveler - (rating 2 out of 5) I met this guy who claimed to be nine inches. But when we got back to my hotel room and I pulled out my traveling ruler—he ran away.

Our Top Traveler - (rating 3 out of 5) I got the greatest put down ever at a bar in New Orleans when I was trying to get this twinkish young guy to go back to my hotel room. After a little sarcastic banter, I asked him, "Are you a real bitch or just a whore?", to which he replied: "I'm a bitch because a whore would let everyone fuck him at this bar. Bitches let everyone fuck them at this bar except you." Then he walked away.

LOUISIANA

ACCOMMODATIONS

The Stockade
8860 Highland Road
Baton Rouge, LA 70808
Tel: (225) 769-7358 | (888) 900-5430
http://www.thestockade.com/

The Stockade is a cozy, hospitable B&B that gives visitors the full Baton Rouge experience. Comfy amenities like antique furnished rooms and southern style breakfasts (not to mention the free Wi-Fi) make The Stockade perfect for romantic couple getaways.

Bourbon Orleans Hotel
717 Orleans Avenue (Between Royal and Bourbon)
New Orleans, LA 70116
French Quarter
Tel: (504) 523-2222 | (866) 513-9744
E-mail: GuestServices@BourbonOrleans.com
http://www.bourbonorleans.com/

This historic hotel provides all the Southern charm one could hope for in New Orleans. Having recently undergone expansive renovations, its French inspired style and elegant rooms remain perhaps unchallenged in the city today.

Hotel St. Pierre
911 Burgundy Street (Dumaine Street)
New Orleans, LA 70116
French Quarter
Tel: (504) 524-4401 | (800) 225-4040
http://www.hotelsaintpierre.com/

The Hotel St. Pierre is a well-known gay-friendly establishment, especially during the Southern Decadence celebrations. It offers a unique style with rooms surrounding courtyards and two luxurious pools.

RESTAURANTS

Clover Grill
900 Bourbon Street (Dumaine Street)
New Orleans, LA 70116
French Quarter
Tel: (504) 598-1010
http://www.clovergrill.com/

Open 24/7

This 24/7 diner is without a doubt the best and most easily
accessible spot to catch a bite in the French Quarter. Perfect for
late-night cravings, the Clover Grill will certainly hit any diner's
sweet spot.

The Court of Two Sisters
613 Royal Street (Between St. Peter and Toulouse)
New Orleans, LA 70130
French Quarter
Tel: (504) 522-7273
Reservation line: (504) 522-7261
E-mail: court2si@courtoftwosisters.com
http://www.courtoftwosisters.com

Daily till 10 p.m.

Located on the famous Royal Street, this classy restaurant offers a
daily jazz brunch buffet. Spontaneous foodies beware: without a
reservation, it's near impossible to get a seat during busy dinner
hours! This shouldn't be dissuading however; it's still definitely
worth a peek or two!

Mestizo
2323 Acadian Thruway
Baton Rouge, LA 70806
Tel: (225) 387-2699
Fax: (225) 387-2696

Open for Lunch & Dinner
Monday - Thursday 11:00 am - 9:30 pm
Friday & Saturday 11:00 am - 10:30 pm
Closed Sunday

Enjoy this apercu taken right off of Mestizo's website: "Welcome to Mestizo, Louisiana- Mexican Restaurant of Baton Rouge. Come in and join us for our unique Mexican dishes, generous drinks and loads of fun in relaxed casual atmosphere. We are located at 2323 S Acadian Thwy right off of I10."

The Bourbon Pub and Parade
801 Bourbon Street (St. Anne Street)
New Orleans, LA 70116
French Quarter
Tel: (504) 529-2107
http://www.bourbonpub.com/

Open 24/7

Any traveler strolling down Bourbon St. will wind up in The Bourbon Pub sooner or later. Hearing the sounds from its vibrant dance floor will sway you to walk in and check out the two bars upstairs and the giant basement video bar.

Oz
800 Bourbon Street (St. Anne Street)
New Orleans, LA 70116
French Quarter
Tel: (504) 593-9491
http://www.ozneworleans.com/

Open 7 days a week

Afterhours seekers will find their all-night dancing fix at Oz. With two floors of dancing, a wide balcony to check out the boys, and some of the best shows on Bourbon St, Oz certainly does not disappoint.

Splash
2183 Highland Rd
Baton Rouge, LA 70802
Tel: (225) 242-9491
contact@splashbr.com
http://www.splashbr.com/

Theme nights are large and abound at this gay-lesbian club. Drop by if you're into drag shows, dancing, and general debauchery!

8. MASSACHUSETTS

Massachusetts was the first state in the United States to legalize same-sex marriages. It is undoubtedly the most progressive state in the United States, with liberal laws dating back to even before the US Civil War.

Massachusetts is a New England haven steeped in US revolutionary war history sites, dating back to when it was a part of the 13 colonies controlled by England. It was the first state to rebel against colonial rule.

Boston is a confusing city to drive in, but once you are there the gay night life is fun and vibrant.

Our Bottom Traveler - (rating 4 out of 5) We walked into this bar and everyone seemed to be having deep intelligent conversations. So, I walked up to this guy and said "small talk, can be about spirituality or politics, or about more important issues like our favorite sex positions." Let's just say that in my hotel room, I got his "point of view" in me.

Our Top Traveler - (rating 5 out of 5) I was surprised at how sexy the guys were in Boston; no one ever says this. I met a great guy who took me home and made me a full brunch setting the next day. He also gave me a tour of the city. He told me that he was a "Unitarian" and I stupidly asked him: "What Slavic country is that?"

MASSACHUSETTS

ACCOMMODATIONS

Oasis Guest House
22 Edgerly Rd. (Haviland St.)
Boston, MA 02115
Back Bay
Tel: (617) 267-2262 | (800) 230-0105
http://www.oasisgh.com/

This small yet quaint guest house caters mostly to gay clients.
Located near the nightlife and shopping of Boston, the Oasis
boasts modest rooms from $79 a night_a solid choice for any
visitor.

Boston Marriott Copley Place
110 Huntington Ave.
Boston, MA 02116
Downtown/North End
Tel: (617) 236-5800
http://www.marriott.com/hotels/travel/bosco-boston

Although not specifically designed for gays, this popular branch
of the famous Marriot Hotels sports a great location near many
shopping malls, including the Copley Place Mall and the
Prudential Center Mall. This makes it a must for avid shoppers!

The Hotel Northampton
36 King St. (Main St.)
Northampton, MA 01060
Downtown
Tel: (413) 584-3100
http://www.hotelnorthampton.com/

Featuring 106 guest rooms and luxury suites, the historic Hotel
Northampton offers visitors an excellent place to relax after
intensive shopping sprees. This hotel's in-house restaurant

(Wiggin's Tavern) is a must visit for seafood lovers and vintage décor enthusiasts!

RESTAURANTS

Stella Restaurant
1525 Washington St. (W. Brookline St.)
Boston, MA 02118
South End
Tel: (617) 247-7747
http://www.bostonstella.com/

Dinner till 2 a.m.

Affordable Italian cuisine in a chic environment is just one of the
reasons to check out this trendy bistro. Its modern dining space
features over-sized windows looking out on a large outdoor
seating area. Late-night munchers rejoice! Their kitchen is open
till 1:30am.

Tremont 647 & Sister Sorel
647 Tremont St. (W. Brookline St.)
Boston, MA 02118
South End
Tel: (617) 266-4600
http://www.tremont647.com/

Dinner till 10 p.m.

This eatery offers a delicious menu of American classics for gay
diners, as well as a special weekend (Sat. and Sun.) treat known
colloquially as "Pajama Brunch".

Paul & Elizabeth's
150 Main St. (Inside Thorne's Market)
Northampton, MA 01060
Downtown
Tel: (413) 584-4832
http://www.paulandelizabeths.com/

Sun. - Thurs., 11 a.m. - 9:15 p.m.

Fri., Sat., 11:30 a.m. - 9:45 p.m.
Sun. Brunch 11 a.m.

Inspired by the natural food movement of the 70's, Paul & Elizabeth's is the best place to try mercury free, all-natural fresh fish (and tempura!). A gorgeous view of Main St. and Old South St. makes this restaurant quite a catch!

Club Café
209 Columbus Ave. (Clarendon St.)
Boston, MA 2216
South End
Tel: (617) 536-0966
http://www.clubcafé.com

Wed-Sat till 1 or 2 a.m.

A notable (and weekend-popular) South End standard for over 27 years, Club Café is located within walking distance from most downtown hotels. With a 3-section layout (Main bar & lounge, backroom bar & dance floor, brand spanking new Napoleon Room piano bar) and plenty of good looking boys to boot, Club Café continues to prove why it's the number one gay club on the South End.

Fritz's Lounge
26 Chandler @Berkley
Street
Boston, MA 02116
Tel: (617) 482-4428

Here's what Fritz's has to say about their lively joint: "The crowd at Fritz is friendly and the staff are always there to make your time more enjoyable. Pull up a chair and watch your favorite sporting events on our high definition satellite system. Fritz has six flat screen plasma TVs located throughout the bar, so you'll always get a prime view."

Diva's Nightclub
492 Pleasant St.
Northampton, MA 01060
Downtown

Tel: (413) 586-8161

http://www.divasofnoho.com

Tues. - Sat. till 2 a.m.

LGBT crowd look no further! Diva's Nightclub is the perfect place for you and whoever else just wants to have fun—they accept all lifestyles! They are renowned for their drag wars as much as for their pumping music and rockin' dance floor!

9. MINNESOTA

Minnesota was once considered a liberal state, but has recently become more conservative. Minnesota has no statutes explicitly banning same sex marriages, but ironically was the first state ever to be sued for gay marriage rights back in 1972.

Minnesota is a nice scenic state with many nature parks. Few people know that this is where the singer Prince comes from. Although Minneapolis is considered a gay hot spot for some, we found that it's truly the men in this state that make Minnesota worth a visit.

Our Bottom Traveler - (rating 4 out of 5) With the right amount of beer, you can have any guy in the bar.

Our Top Traveler - (rating 4 out of 5) With the right amount of beer, you can have EVERY guy in the bar.

MINNESOTA

ACCOMMODATIONS

Graves 601 Hotel
601 First Ave. North
Minneapolis, MN 55403
Downtown Minneapolis
Tel: (612) 677-1100 | (866) 523-1100
http://www.graves601hotel.com/

This critically acclaimed hotel is definitely worth checking out.
Dubbed as "the hottest and most fashionable" hotel in
Minneapolis by the New York Times, and making Condé Nast's
gold List and Travel & Leisure's best business hotel list are just
two indications of this hotel's satisfying experience.

Crowne Plaza Hotel
618 2nd Ave. S. (6th St.)
Minneapolis, MN 55402
Downtown Minneapolis

Tel: (612) 338-2288 | (187) 742-4422
http://www.ichotelsgroup.com/crowneplaza/hotels/us/en/minneap
olis/mspcp/hoteldetail?rpb=hotel&crUrl=/h/d/cp/1/en/hotelsearch
results

The Minneapolis branch of this hotel chain lives up to the name
of "Crowne Plaza". It's conveniently located near shopping and
nightlife. Rooms run around $150/night.

Olcott House Bed & Breakfast
2316 East 1st Street
Duluth, MN 55812
Downtown
Tel: (218) 728-1339 | (800) 715-1339
http://www.olcotthouse.com/

This quaint B&B is perfect for any romantic couple, being located just minutes from Lake Superior. Featuring delicious food with a myriad of vegetarian options as well as in-room spa treatments, the Olcott House will surely not disappoint.

RESTAURANTS

Hell's Kitchen
80 South 9th St.
Minneapolis, MN 55403
Downtown Minneapolis
Tel: (612) 332-4700
http://www.hellskitcheninc.com

6:30am-9pm

Though Hell's Kitchen serves food for all meals, its breakfast
dishes are what really make it shine. Try the Lemon Ricotta
Pancakes, Huevos Rancheros, and Bloody Marys; all local
favorites. Miss the breakfast rush? With a 3-6pm happy hour and
a heavenly Sunday brunch (with a great gospel music
soundtrack), Hell's Kitchen is a great find.

Wilde Roast Café
518 Hennepin Ave. E (Central Ave.)
Minneapolis, MN 55414
St. Anthony Main
Tel: 612.331.4544
Fax: 612.331.1130
Email: oscar@wilderoastcafé.com
http://www.wilderoastcafé.com

Open 7am - 10pm daily

This Victorian-inspired Café, named for playwright Oscar Wilde,
features a full menu of traditional Minnesota comfort
foods—perfect for everyone's taste.

Pizza Luce
11 East Superior Street
Duluth, MN 55802
Downtown
Tel: (218) 727-7400
http://www.pizzaluce.com

8am-1:30am

Don't let the collegiate atmosphere of this Duluth pizza joint fool you; the live music and delicious pizza make it a great stop for all ages. Be sure to check out their weekend brunch menu for a delicious Duluth experience.

NIGHTLIFE

The Saloon
830 Hennepin Ave. (9th & Hennepi)
Minneapolis, MN 55403
Downtown Minneapolis
Tel: (612) 332-0835
http://www.saloonmn.com

12pm-2am, Open till 3am Thu-Sat

This popular dance bar has the standard features that one might
expect: a dance floor, video bar, outdoor patio, and back bar that
attracts a leather-donning crowd on Sundays. Packed with
younger clients and high energy music, this bar is a must visit for
energetic party goers. The Saloon is 18+ on Thursdays and
Saturdays, with Go-go boys on Sundays, Wednesdays and
Fridays.

Gay 90s
408 Hennepin Avenue (4th St.)
Minneapolis, MN 55401
Downtown Minneapolis
Tel: (612) 333-7755
http://www.gay90s.com/

9pm-2am, Open for Dinner at 5pm

As evidenced by its revealing name, this pro-gay establishment is
one of the largest in Minneapolis. It features three dance floors,
two restaurants, eight bars (including a leather bar), drag shows,
and male strippers. Though pro-gay, this club draws a varied
crowd, so clubbers can expect to mingle with straight singles on
busy nights as well.

19 Bar
19 W. 15th St. (Nicolet)
Minneapolis, MN 55403
Loring Park
Tel: (612) 871-5553

http://19bar.itgo.com/

3pm-2am Daily

The oldest gay bar in the twin cities caters to men of all ages.
Visitors can expect to find a diverse range of party goers, from
older business men to younger college students.
Bar-games abound, this bar features favorites such as darts and
pool.

10. New York

New York is undoubtedly where the gay rights movement took off with the infamous 1969 Stonewall Riots. The first Gay Liberation March was held in 1970, and is known today worldwide as Gay Pride. New York has a rich history of accepting LGBT rights and recognitions; and now, thanks to Governor Cuomo, on June 24, 2011 same-sex unions were legalized in New York.

New York City is the NUMBER ONE gay tourist attraction in the world, and will forever be etched into history as pioneering the rights of the LGBT Community.

Our Bottom Traveler - (rating 5 out of 5) There is this misconception that New York has the most top men in the USA. I would say there are a lot but not the most. If you are a bottom, this is a good place to go, and you don't have to put in a lot of effort to find a HUNG top.

Our Top Traveler - (rating 5 out of 5) We stayed an extra week *just* so that I could see how many nationalities I could sleep with in one city. New York is just a menu of different cultures.

NEW YORK

ACCOMMODATIONS

Chelsea Pines Inn
317 W 14th Street (Between 8th and 9th Ave)
New York, NY 10014
Chelsea

Tel: (212) 929-1023 | (888) 546-2700
http://www.chelseapinesinn.com/

This 5-story converted private home is an iconic haunt at the heart of Gay New York. Hung all throughout the interior of this inn (in private rooms as well) are famous posters from iconic films of the Golden Age of Hollywood. Visitors will be delighted at the 300 thread-count luxury linens and Gilchrist & Soames bath soaps as well.

Colonial House Inn
318 W. 22nd St. (Between 8th & 9th Avenues)
New York, NY 10011
Chelsea
Tel: (212) 243-9669 | (800) 689-3779
http://www.colonialhouseinn.com/

Another historic hospice in the heart of Gay New York, Colonial House Inn's central location in Chelsea makes it perfect for travelers pent on exploring the city. Established in 1985, this inn has held great importance for the local gay community: it is most well-known for being the home of the Gay Men's Health Crisis. All rooms are non-smoking and complimentary breakfast is served from 7:00am-10:00am daily.

Holiday Inn Downtown
620 Delaware Avenue
Buffalo, NY 14202

Tel: (716) 886-2121 | (800) 465-4329
http://www.holidayinn.com/h/d/hi/1/en/hotel/BUFMT/welcome?start=1

This Holiday Inn's convenient location at the center of gay Allentown makes it a good choice for the economical traveler. It's also conveniently located within walking distance of Buffalo's nightlife, shopping, and restaurants.

RESTAURANTS

Elmo
156 Seventh Ave.
Between 20th & 19th
New York City
Tel: (212) 337-8000
Fax : (212) 242-0612
http://www.elmorestaurant.com

Elmo is the top choice for trendy-conscious travelers. Its classy
lounge, fashionable environment, diverse menu, and nightly
basement entertainment will keep visitors constantly coming back
for more.

Vynl Hell's Kitchen
754 Ninth Avenue (51st Street)
New York, NY 10019
Hell's Kitchen
Tel: (212) 974-2003
http://www.vynl-nyc.com/

Mon-Wed 11am-11pm,
Thurs-Fri: 11am-1am,
Sat/Sun: 9:30-1am (11pm on Sunday)

'Kitschy' is the best word to describe this Hell's Kitchen favorite.
Vynl's features delectable American-Thai cuisine and elaborate
displays of celebrity dolls, with famous faces such as Britney,
Donnie & Marie, and Sonny & Cher. For diners wanting a little
drink with their food, ask the skilled bartenders to mix whatever
your heart desires—they will most certainly oblige.

Betty's
370 Virginia Street
Buffalo, NY 14201

Tel: (716) 362-0633
E-mail: bettysbuffalo@gmail.com
http://www.bettysbuffalo.com/

Closed Mondays

Betty's is a solid choice for the Buffalo traveler. It has a charming
atmosphere and a diverse, vegetarian friendly menu to
boot—great for everyone's palate.

NIGHTLIFE

Splash
50 W 17th St (Between 5th & 6th Ave.)
New York, NY 10011
Chelsea
Tel: (212) 691-0073
http://www.splashbar.com

Gay tourists are implored to visit this locally renowned club.
Attractions such as large video screens, hot bartenders, strong
drinks, and lots of sexy dancing ensure that the Splash lives up to
its hype. College-aged visitors will delight every Thursday, where
a college ID will net a free cover charge.

The Monster
80 Grove St. (Sheridan Sq)
New York, NY 10014
West Village
Tel: (212) 924-3558
http://www.manhattan-monster.com

Nestled in the infamous West Village, The Monster will
definitely impress. Its multiple levels include a 1st floor piano bar
and rockin' basement dance floor. Come for the friendly crowd,
stay for the entertainment—fabulous drag shows and wonderful
singers.

Club Marcella
622 Main Street
Buffalo, NY 14202
Tel: (716) 847-6850
clubmarcella@gmail.com
http://www.clubmarcella.com/Club_Marcella/home.html

Known for its energetic drag shows, Club Marcella is a great
choice on a weekend night. If you're looking to mingle with non-
gays, this club is certainly the place for you. For traditional drag,

stop by on a Sunday; other nights tend to feature drag in its more "alternative" forms.

11. North Carolina

North Carolina is one of a handful of states that has not repealed their anti-sodomy laws. Although rendered unenforceable by the US Supreme Court in 2003, these laws are still on the books in the state.

North Carolina has no official state recognition of same sex relationships in any form. The statutes limit marriage to one man and one woman. There are no anti-discrimination laws protecting the LGBT Community.

North Carolina is given an "F" grade for failure as being the worst of all the states reviewed in this book in terms of LGBT rights.

Our Bottom Traveler - (rating 5 out of 5) This is hands down the state with the most Tops. I had no trouble finding a willing top that was eager to please.

Our Top Traveler - (rating 2 out of 5) So, after sex, this guy had the nerve to tell me that he was not gay. To which I replied: "Oh please, that pounding sensation you just felt in your ass tells me that you are."

NORTH CAROLINA

ACCOMMODATIONS

Courtyard Charlotte City Center
237 S. Tryon Street
Charlotte, NC 28202
Uptown
Tel: (704) 926-5800
Fax: (704) 926-5801
Sales Tel: (704) 926-5804
Sales Fax: (704) 926-5809
Toll-free: 1-888-839-1758
http://www.marriott.com/hotels/travel/cltup-courtyard-charlotte-city-center/

Read for yourself what Marriot has to say about their Charlotte branch: "With attractive and comfortable guest room accommodations, the Courtyard by Marriott Charlotte City Center hotel is sure to meet your needs. Located in the heart of Charlotte's uptown financial and entertainment district, our Charlotte NC hotel is perfect for both business and leisure travel."

Morehead Inn
1122 E. Morehead Street
Charlotte, NC 28204
Tel: (704) 376-3357
Fax: (704) 335-1110 fax
Toll-free: 1-888-667-3432
http://www.moreheadinn.com/

Check out this description courtesy of the Morehead: "The Morehead Inn is located just minutes from Uptown Charlotte in one of the city's most picturesque neighborhoods. An elegant Southern estate endowed with quiet elegance and fine antiques, our spacious and historic Dilworth home features intimate fireplaces, luxurious private guest rooms and a lovely four-bedroom carriage house."

The Umstead Hotel and Spa
100 Woodland Pond Drive
Cary, NC 27513
Toll Free: (866) 877-4141
Local Tel: (919) 447-4000
guestservices@theumstead.com
http://www.theumstead.com/

As viewable on their website: "The Umstead Hotel and Spa was conceived and built with the muses of Art and Nature. These inspirations paired with impeccable, sincere service make for an exquisite hideaway that will comfort and rejuvenate. Everything – from the naturally landscaped grounds to the central Chihuly glass sculpture, our locally sourced cuisine to our botanically infused Umstead Spa products – is designed to stir the senses and inspire."

RESTAURANTS

300 East
300 East Blvd.
Charlotte, NC 28203
Southend

Tel: (704) 332-6507
http://300east.net

According to their website: "Within a renovated house in historic
Dilworth, 300 East serves inspired cuisine in a lively, offbeat and
relaxed atmosphere. In this unique setting, neighborhood
residents come for a grass fed burger at the bar, families gather
for special occasions in the upstairs dining room, couples enjoy a
quiet dinner in a tiny secluded booth and friends share wine and
appetizers on the shady patio facing East Boulevard."

Common Market
2007 Commonwealth Ave
Charlotte, NC 28205
Plaza Midwood
Tel: (704) 334-6209
info@commonmarketisgood.com
http://www.commonmarketisgood.com/

This down-to-earth deli may be the best place to grab a delicious
sandwich in Charlotte. Stop by sometime and hope you are lucky
enough to hear some of their live music events!

The Borough
317 West Morgan St. (Dawson)
Raleigh, NC 27603
Tel: (919) 832-8433
http://www.theboroughraleigh.com/
Free Wi-Fi access

Open 7 days a week from 4pm to 2am
Monday-Friday 4 to 7pm: 1/2-priced appetizers

As self-described on their site: "The Borough is one of the best bars in Raleigh! The staff is amazing - the place can be PACKED (and it usually is) but the service doesn't slow down. The food is delicious. The crowd is always fun and friendly. It's good for groups, so bring all of your friends!"

Sidelines
4544 South Blvd. (Behind Skyland Restaurant)
Charlotte, NC 28209
Southend
Tel: (704) 525-2608
http://www.thesidelinesbar.com/

Daily 4pm-2am (from Noon Sat/Sun)

Here's what Sidelines says they have to offer: "Sidelines Sports
Bar and Billiards is a unique, friendly, and accepting place to
relax. You can enjoy a cold beer, a great drink, a Martini, or one
of our seven draft beers. With 13 TV's you are able to watch your
favorite sporting events. You can play a FREE game of pool or
Wii. Also available is darts and Wi-Fi."

The Scorpio
2301 Freedom Dr.
Charlotte, NC 28208
Tel: (704) 373-9124
http://www.scorpios.com

Check out this great description by The Scorpio: "The Scorpio is
Charlotte's longest running nightclub complex (43 years) catering
to the gay/lesbian/bisexual/Transgender community. Our doors
are open to all. The Scorpio is located at 2301 Freedom Drive and
is open Wednesdays, Friday, Saturday and Sunday at 10 PM -
2:30AM."

Legends
330 W. Hargett St.
Raleigh, NC 27601
Tel: (919) 831-8888
manager@legends-club.com
http://www.legends-club.com/

Open daily until 2 AM

Here's what Legends has to say about themselves: "A private club catering to the Triangle's GLBT community. Legends Nightclub Complex is proud to feature the Best New Dance Tracks, the Finest in Female Impersonation, and Live Entertainment!"

12. OHIO

Ohio has very few LGBT rights compared to more progressive states in the country. Surprisingly though, Ohio repealed their anti-sodomy laws in 1972. Since 2004, there has been an Ohio State Issue prohibiting the recognition, on the state level, of same-sex marriages.

Discrimination against the LGBT Community Is prohibited only within the Ohio State Government.

Our Bottom Traveler - (rating 3 out of 5) We went to about 3 cities in Ohio and found that they all had really nice tight-knit gay communities. I was actually invited to a potluck dinner after hooking up with a guy. This was a first and a pleasant surprise.

Our Top Traveler - (rating 3 out of 5) I think Ohio has the dumbest gay men that I ever met. This guy said he was a rent boy and had made $47.50 that night. So I asked him which guy gave him the $0.50 cents. To which he replied, "All of them."

OHIO

ACCOMMODATIONS

Residence Inn Downtown Columbus
36 E. Gay Street
Columbus, OH 43215
Downtown
Tel: (614) 222-2610
http://www.marriott.com/cmhrd

Features of this conveniently located downtown high-rise include rooms with fully equipped kitchens, living and work areas, and complimentary wired or Wi-Fi Internet.

The Westin Columbus
310 South High Street
Columbus, OH 43215
Tel: (614) 228-3800
Toll Free: 1-800-937-8461
http://www.westincolumbus.com/

European-style enthusiasts will delight at The Westin's French Renaissance elegance and décor. Operating since 1897, this hotel is perfect for guests who value history and charm.

Flex Hotel, Spa & Gym
2600 Hamilton Ave. (St. Claire & E. 26th St.)
Cleveland, OH 44114
St. Clair/Superior
Tel: (216) 812-3304
http://www.flexbaths.com/content/view/121/323/

Clean and pamper yourself after a hot night out at this gorgeous spa. Choose Flex for its in-house gym, Quiet Spa Rooms, and Grand Presidential Suites—complete with a grand piano.

RESTAURANTS

Level Dining Lounge
700 North High Street
Columbus, OH 43215
Short North
Tel: (614) 754-7111
http://www.levelcolumbus.com

Diners looking for a chic yet laid back atmosphere will delight at
this lounge's menu, catered towards the highly refined palate.

Union Café
782 N High St
Columbus, OH 43215
Short North
Tel: (614) 421-2233
http://www.unioncafé.com/

This web-blurb sums Union Café up nicely: "Union Café is one
of Columbus' most popular neighborhood cafés and cocktail
lounges, serving the community since 1996. With an amazing
patio, friendly staff, mind-bending martini menu and Modern
American Cuisine served at popular prices, Union Café is
affordable and welcoming."

Luxe
6605 Detroit Ave. (W. 67th St.)
Cleveland, OH 44102
Detroit Shoreway
Tel: (216) 920-0600
http://www.luxecleveland.com

The heavily gay neighborhood of Detroit Shoreway adds to the
allure of this fancy bistro.
Featuring a heated patio and live music, Luxe is quickly
becoming one of Cleveland's most popular gay hangouts.

Exile
893 N. 4th St
Columbus, OH 43201
Italian Village
Tel: (614) 299-0069
http://www.exilebar.com/

Tues - Sat 4 pm - 2:30 am
Sun 2 pm - 2:30 am
Closed Mondays

This leather-themed bar, featuring leather competitions, strippers, and brick-wall décor, is perfect for the leather fanatic. Pop in on Sundays for the Bloody Marys and Mimosas at their "Liquid Brunch".

Axis
775 N. High St.
Columbus, OH 43215
Short North
Tel: (614) 228-4008
http://www.columbusnightlife.com/unioncafé2010/index.php?tabid=33

Frequented by students from OSU, Axis is perfect for those who want to flirt with the college boys. And if that wasn't enough to satiate your appetite, the dominant mix of techno and house music will keep you dancing all night long.

A Man's World Complex
2909 Detroit Ave. (W. 29th St.)
Cleveland, OH 44113
Tel: (216) 589-9322
http://www.amwcomplex.com/

Daily from 11 a.m.

With 3 bars in its repertoire (Men's World, The Shed, The Crossover), this club/bar/restaurant complex has something to satisfy everyone. An upstairs dance club, mid-floor lounge, and downstairs leather bar makes sure that everyone goes home with something happy. The event seeker will delight at Men's World's bi-gender "Rainbow Wranglers" country line dancing, held Sundays at 6 p.m.

13. PENNSYLVANIA

Pennsylvania did not fully repeal their anti-sodomy laws until 1995. Pennsylvania does not recognizes same-sex marriages, civil unions, or domestic partnerships in any form, which was put into place by a state statute.

The state did have an anti-discrimination law but it was struck down by the Pennsylvania State Supreme Court in 2008 on a technicality. Efforts have been made to reinstate the revised statute, but have failed to pass in the legislature.

Our Bottom Traveler - (rating 2 out of 5) This was the first time that a guy had the nerve to ask my age. I told him that I am fearless about fighting the elements, especially gravity....but don't ask my age. It was also the first time that I learned that "bad ass" was meant as a compliment.

Our Top Traveler - (rating 3 out of 5). This gay club we went to was so sketchy that even a dwarf would've gotten pick pocketed. How could anyone stoop so low? It's here that I also coined the term "Gay Dumb" because this guy I took home was so "Gay Dumb" he thought the "Super Bowl" required a spoon.

PENNSYLVANIA

ACCOMMODATIONS

Alexander Inn
301 South 12th Street (Spruce)
Philadelphia, PA 19107
Washington Square West
Tel: (215) 923-3535 | (877) 253-9466
http://www.alexanderinn.com/

Reasonable rates from $129/night, comfortable stylish rooms, and a location within walking distance of Philly's nightlife: 3 reasons why the Alexander is a great choice for accommodation.

Loews Philadelphia
1200 Market Street
Philadelphia, PA 19107
Chinatown
Tel: (215) 627-1200 | (888) 575-6397
http://www.loewshotels.com/philadelphia

The Loews Philadelphia certainly has some history behind it: it's located in the first skyscraper ever built in Philly! This stylish hotel chain lives up to its name in every way imaginable, from amazing rooms to generous amenities.

Arbors Bed & Breakfast
745 Maginn St.
Pittsburgh, PA 15214
North Side
Tel: (412) 231-4643
http://www.arborsbnb.com/

This gay-owned B&B is cozy, comfy, and quaint; perfect for the gay traveling couple! Located 15-minutes driving distance from downtown, charming rooms start at just $115/night. For larger groups, a whole-house rental option is available as well.

Venture Inn
255 S. Camac Street
Philadelphia, PA 19107
Washington Square West
Tel: (215) 545-8731
http://www.viphilly.com

Located right in the middle of historic Philadelphia, the Venture Inn is perfect for taking in the buildings around you or for setting up a historic trip to parts of the Underground Railroad.

RESTAURANTS

Eleven
1150 Smallman St
Pittsburgh, PA 15222
Strip District
Tel: (412) 201-5656
http://www.bigburrito.com/eleven

The Pittsburgh Gazette says: "The food is amazing, the presentation is gorgeous, the wine list impressive, and the interior classy", giving Eleven an impressive 4 stars.

Point Brugge Café
401 Hastings St
Pittsburgh, PA 15206
Shadyside
Tel: (412) 441-3334
http://www.pointbrugge.com

Check out this blurb from pointbrugge.com: "Point Brugge Café opened in the Point Breeze neighborhood of Pittsburgh's East End in January 2005. Its Belgian-inspired cuisine, fresh ingredients and reasonable pricing made it an instant hit with the neighborhood and beyond. Point Brugge is consistently rated one of the top restaurants in the area by major publications and social media sites."

Woody's
202 S. 13th St. (Walnut)
Philadelphia, PA 19107
Washington Square West
Tel: (215) 545-1893
http://www.woodysbar.com/

Daily 11am-2am

How can you go wrong with a name like Woody's? A wide
selection of rooms cater to the many faces of Philadelphia's gay
crowd. Whether you're looking for a bar, pub, or club atmosphere
(or even a Café Latte at a Coffee bar), Woody's has something
for everyone.

The Bike Stop
206 S. Quince St.
(Between 11th & 12th Sts and Walnut & Locust Sts)
Philadelphia, PA 19107
Washington Square West
Tel: (215) 627-1662
http://www.thebikestop.com/
Mon-Fri 4pm-2am
Sat-Sun 2pm-2am

A multi-tiered establishment, The Bike Stop offers entertainment
for all varieties of clientele. Be it dancing on the 3rd floor,
catching the game on the 2nd, cruising on the 1st, or toiling in
some basement leather, The Bike Stop satisfies all curiosities. Be
sure to check out their live music every Sunday night!

5801 Video Lounge & Café
5801 Ellsworth Ave. (Maryland)
Pittsburgh, PA 15232
Shadyside
Tel: (412) 661-5600
http://www.5801.us/

Daily 4pm-2am
Open 12:30 pm for Sunday Steeler's games and occasionally
open for Sunday brunch at 11 am.

Video lovers unite! This rather upscale lounge features large
video screens playing new hits and old classics alike. Sporting a
large outdoor eating area and daily drink specials, the 5801 is a
must visit for any gay visitor to Pittsburg.

14. TEXAS

Texas has long been a center of legal activity regarding LGBT rights. Although Texas lost its case before the US Supreme Court in terms of their sodomy laws in 2003, the Texas Health and Safety Code still mandates that, "The materials in the education programs intended for persons younger than 18 years of age must...state that homosexual conduct is not an acceptable lifestyle and is a criminal offense under §21.06 of the Penal Code."

The general conclusion by our author and two travelers is that Texas gets a "D" grade in terms of gay tourism. The ONLY bright spot in Texas is Dallas. Our travelers found the city to be a lot of fun and vibrant.

Our Bottom Traveler - (rating 5 out of 5) In texas, you need the finish the sentence with: "Everything is BIG in Texas (with the help of VIAGRA)" J.

Our Top Traveler - (rating 2 out of 5) Dallas was a fun city, but Ft. Worth and Houston totally were unwelcoming and boring. When they ask if you have a pistol in your pocket, it's the only place where they REALLY mean a pistol.

ACCOMMODATIONS

Warwick Melrose Hotel, Dallas
3015 Oak Lawn Ave.
Dallas, TX 75219
Oaklawn
Tel: (214) 521-5151 | (800) 635-7673
http://www.warwickmelrosedallas.com/

As listed on their website: "Setting the standard among luxury
hotels in Dallas, the Four-Diamond AAA awarded Warwick
Melrose Hotel offers an unmatched level of grandeur and
comfort. Built in 1924, this historic landmark is home to 184
deluxe guest rooms, including 20 suites and a Presidential Suite.
This stylish hotel is set in one of Dallas' most fashionable
neighborhoods, offering a great location as well as a touch of
stately grandeur."

Daisy Polk Inn
2917 Reagan St.
Dallas, TX 75219
Oaklawn
Tel: (214) 522-4692
http://www.daisypolkinn.com/

Quaint and cozy define this inn. Gay-owned and sporting three
delightful rooms, the Daisy Polk Inn is an excellent choice for
cozy bungalow lovers.

InterContinental Stephen F. Austin Hotel
701 Congress Avenue
Austin, TX 78701
Warehouse District
Tel: (512) 457-8800
http://www.austin.intercontinental.com/

Taken from the Austin's website: "The choice for luxury in downtown Austin, the InterContinental Stephen F.
Austin provides lodging just four blocks from the Austin State Capitol and puts you within walking distance of the Bob Bullock Texas State History Museum, the University of Texas and the Lady Bird Lake Hike and Bike Trail."

RESTAURANTS

Hunky's
4000 Cedar Springs Road
Dallas, Tx 75219
Oaklawn
Tel: (214) 522-1212
http://www.hunkys.com/

11am-10pm

Burgers and Texas seem to be a fantastic combination that never gets old. Stop by Hunky's for old-fashioned milkshakes, fries, and other good ol' American classics.

Buli Café
3908 Cedar Springs Rd
Dallas, TX 75219
Oaklawn
Tel: (214) 528-5410
http://bulicafé.com/

7am-midnight

Here's what the Buli Café has to say about itself: "Enjoy the most eclectic coffee bar in Dallas. Fabulous breakfast sandwiches, fresh baked muffins, scones, tarts, bagels and breads. And grab a panini lunch box to go!"

Santa Rita Cantina
1206 West 38th Street
Austin, TX 78705
Capitol
Tel: (512) 419-7482

http://www.santaritacantina.com/

Here's a delicious blurb, courtesy of Santa Rita: "In a time before the Beatles, Doña Margarita B. achieved considerable culinary acclaim along the Rio Bravo from the chile plantations of New Mexico to the ranchos grandes of the Gulf coast. To this day, she is considered by many to be the Mother of (All) Tex-Mex."

NIGHTLIFE

Round-Up Saloon
3912 Cedar Springs Rd.
Dallas, TX 75219
Oaklawn
Tel: (214) 522-9611
http://www.roundupsaloon.com/

3pm-2am

You wanted it, you got it: A country & western themed, gay dance club in the heart of Oaklawn. The Round-Up Saloon perfectly sates the country music lover. Just take it from Instinct Magazine, who named round up saloon "The Best Galdanged Gay Bar in the U.S. of A".

Station 4
3911 Cedar Springs Rd. (Throckmorton)
Dallas, TX 75219
Oaklawn
Tel: (214) 526-7171
http://www.partyattheblock.com

Wed-Sun 9pm-4am

One of the latest open clubs in Dallas, this joint's 4am closing time makes sure that the party will go on and on till the break of dawn. Check out their Granite bar or the fabulous Krystal Summers and friends at the Rose Room. Station 4 doesn't disappoint!

Oilcan Harry's
211 W 4th St. (Lavaca)
Austin, TX 78701
Warehouse District
Tel: (512) 320-8823
http://www.oilcanharrys.com

Daily 2pm-2am

Geared towards the younger Austin crowd, Oilcan Harry's is often packed from Thursdays-Sundays. With frequent go-go boy shows and a convenient location near other Warehouse District gay bars, you can ogle and hop to your heart's content.

15. WASHINGTON STATE

The State of Washington is now the seventh state to allow gay marriage. Before, they had a state registered domestic partnership program but with the passage of the new law, marriage will be granted to the LGBT community effective June 2012.

The state has anti-discrimination laws and hate crime legislation that protect the LGBT community.

Our two travelers found Seattle to be a fun, friendly, and vibrant city for gay travelers. However, they also fell in love with the quaint city of Bellingham, which is two hours to the north of Seattle. Washington State is a very gay-friendly place and within time will grant full rights to the LGBT community.

Our Bottom Traveler - (rating 5 out of 5) So, we went back to my hotel and this guy said: "I will offer you oral sex or anal sex; but not both." So I asked, "Which are you better at doing?" To which he replied: "My oral sex will make your day but anal sex will make your hole weak!" I think you KNOW which one I picked.

Our Top Traveler - (rating 2 out of 5) So this guy said to me, "Make love to me like in the movies." So I fucked him in the ass, pulled out, and came all over his face and hair. He wasn't very pleased. I guess we don't watch the same movies.

WASHINGTON

ACCOMMODATIONS

W Seattle
1112 Fourth Ave.
Seattle, WA 98101
Downtown
Tel: (206) 264-6000
http://www.whotels.com/seattle

The W Seattle does not disappoint, maintaining the high standard of luxury service one might expect from the W chain. Located near all of Seattle's best hotspots, the W Seattle also contains the critically acclaimed restaurant Earth & Ocean—a must try for the food lover.

Gaslight Inn
1727 15th Ave.
Seattle, WA 98122
Capitol Hill
Tel: (206) 325-3654
http://www.gaslight-inn.com/

According to their website: "The Gaslight Inn is conveniently located on Capitol Hill, Seattle's most exciting neighborhood that also happens to be closest to the center of the city and only about 20 minutes North from the airport. All of Seattle's main attractions including Pike Place Market, are either in walking distance, a short taxi ride or a metro bus ride away."

Courtyard Tacoma Downtown
1515 Commerce Street
Tacoma, Washington
98402 USA
Phone: (253) 591-9100
Fax: (253) 591-9101
Sales: (253) 591-9100 ext. 6584
Sales fax: (253) 591-9101
http://www.marriott.com/hotels/travel/seatd-courtyard-tacoma-

downtown/

Check out this fine description of the Tacoma: "This urban chic hotel is ideally located just across from the Tacoma Convention and Trade Center, in the heart of Tacoma's financial and theater districts. Guests will find much to enjoy at nearby waterfront museums and renowned restaurants."

The Grill on Broadway
314 Broadway East (Thomas St.)
Seattle, WA 98102
Capitol Hill
Tel: (206) 328-7000
http://broadwaygrillseattle.com/

Mon-Thur: 11AM – 1AM
Fri: 11AM – 2AM
Sat: 9AM – 2AM
Sun: 9AM – 10PM

Located on scenic Broadway, this neighborhood grill sports a
diverse menu suitable for anyone's palate. Locals love their
Sunday brunch, and its location at the heart of Seattle's gay scene
isn't too shabby either!

Julia's (on Broadway)
300 Broadway E.
Seattle, WA 98122
Capitol Hill
Tel: (206) 860-1818
http://juliasrestaurantseattle.com/
bigkarsten@aol.com

Sun-Thurs 8am-11pm
Fri-Sat 8am-midnight

As best put by the restaurant itself: "For over 25 years Julia's
chefs have used the freshest local ingredients of the highest
quality. We prepare all of our menu selections fresh from scratch
with an emphasis on giving you the best value and a unique
dining experience."

Ravenous
785 Broadway
Tacoma, WA 98402
Tel: (253) 572-6374
http://www.ravenoustacoma.com/

Boasting a 16 year run in the restaurant business, Ravenous is devilishly famous for their extensive (and delicious) selection of wines. Stop by for a classy evening of wine and a meal, or simply a nice evening out.

The Cuff Complex
1533 13th Ave. (Pine)
Seattle, WA 98122
Capitol Hill
Tel: (206) 323-1525
http://www.cuffcomplex.com/

Daily 2 p.m.-2 a.m. (until 3 a.m. on Friday-Saturday)

A popular destination for manly men, this complex hosts a variety of fun establishments. When choosing The Cuff it's best to go by the following maxim: "Early in the night, tough and old; late in the night, young and bold."

Neighbours
1509 Broadway (Pike (enter through alley on Pike)
Seattle, WA 98122
Capitol Hill
Tel: (206) 324-5358
http://www.neighboursnightclub.com/

Daily until 2 a.m., until 4 a.m. Friday-Saturday
Closed Mondays

Here's what Neighbours has to say on their site: "Neighbours Nightclub opened its doors Labor Day Weekend in 1983 and has become one of Seattle's longest running and largest GLBT nightclubs that can hold cover 1100 people- boasting three levels, a newly expanded lounge- with full food service, a state of the art sound system and light show, and one of the largest dance floors in Seattle."

Vibe Bar & Grill
226 1st Avenue South (W Titus St)
Kent, WA 98032
(Tacoma)
Tel: (253) 852-0815
http://thevibebarandgrill.com/

Vibe is Kent's answer to the growing amount of hip-hop
enthusiasts in the town. With a street-urban attitude and booming
Top 40 hits, Vibe is perhaps the most bumpin' joint in all of Kent.

Icon Empire Press

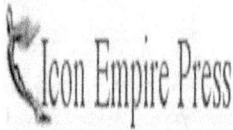

Like us on facebook
www.facebook.com/iconempirepress

ourwebsite: www.gaybooks.info

Other books by Icon Empire Press:
The Gay Icon Contemporary Short Stories by Robert Joseph
Greene
(ISBN 9780986929762)

This collection of iconic contemporary short stories is a series of
male experiences with varying degrees of depth. It looks at the
gay experience within the frame of modern day living, and
connects us with a certain understanding of the human heart.

The Gay Icon Classics Of The World by Robert Joseph Greene
(ISBN 9780986929755)

This book contains a wonderful collection of gay short fiction
fables from around the world. The creation of these stories were
based upon the cultural insights of gay men in history and in
cultures where gay life is taboo. This is a must read for people
who are interested in gaining an understanding of gays from
different cultures and our common search for love.

Icon Empire Press

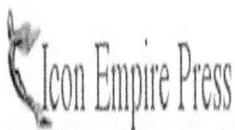

This High School Has Closets
(ISBN <u>9781927124048)</u>

Sometimes coming out during high school just isn't an option.
For Mark Thomas, finding out that he was gay, falling in love,
and dealing with becoming an adult made it even tougher. High
school is a challenge. "This High School Has Closets" is a story
of two young teenagers falling in love during a difficult senior
year.

CROSSOVER II: Straight Men – Gay Encounters
(ISBN <u>9781468072341)</u>

This is the expanded print book from the successful eBook which
addresses the psychological struggle men go through in dealing
with their desire or curiosity with same sex encounters.
CROSSOVER II: Straight Men – Gay Encounters is a collection
of short stories that shows what it's like before, during, and after
such encounters occur.